# A BOOK OF
# Fairies

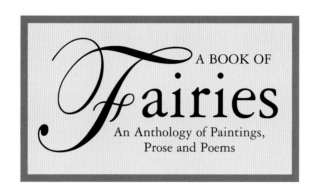

# A BOOK OF
# Fairies

An Anthology of Paintings,
Prose and Poems

Edited by Christine O'Brien

LORENZ BOOKS

This edition is published by Lorenz Books, an imprint of Anness Publishing Ltd, Blaby Road, Wigston, Leicestershire LE18 4SE; info@anness.com

www.lorenzbooks.com; www.annesspublishing.com

Anness Publishing has a new picture agency outlet for images for publishing, promotions or advertising. Please visit our website www.practicalpictures.com for more information.

Editorial Director: Joanna Lorenz
Project Editor: Joanne Rippin
Consultant Editor: Christine O'Brien
Designer: Janet James

## PUBLISHER'S NOTE
Although the advice and information in this book are believed to be accurate and true at the time of going to press, neither the authors nor the publisher can accept any legal responsibility or liability for any errors or omissions that may have been made nor for any inaccuracies nor for any loss, harm or injury that comes about from following instructions or advice in this book.

# Contents

# CHAPTER ONE

# Famous Fairies

*From the romantic legends of medieval Europe to
the children's stories of more recent times,
certain fairies have attracted a wide following and
have been the subject of many adventures.
Among the best-known are Oberon, and Titania the
king and queen of the fairies, Robin
Goodfellow, the merry mischief-
maker, and the
tiny Tom Thumbe.*

I know a bank where the wild thyme blows,
Where oxlips and the nodding violet grows;
Quite overcanopied with lush woodbine,
With sweet musk-roses, and with englantine:
There sleeps Titania some time of the night,
Lull'd in these flowers with dances and delight;
And there the snake throws her enamell'd skin,
Weed wide enough to wrap a fairy in:

WILLIAM SHAKESPEARE (1564-1616) from *A Midsummer Night's Dream*

# ROBIN GOODFELLOW

In the sixteenth century the best-known
English fairy was Robin Goodfellow, also known as
Puck. Supposedly the son of Oberon and a
country woman, he was granted special powers by his
father, who said that he was only to use them
to help honest people. Robin did not always keep to this
condition, however, and he was
as famous for his mischievous
tricks as for washing the
dishes and sweeping the floor.

I am that merry wanderer of the night:
I jest to Oberon, and make him smile,
When I a fat and bean-fed horse beguile,
Neighing in likeness of a filly foal:
And some time lurk I in a gossip's bowl,
In very likeness of a roasted crab;
And when she drinks, against her lips I bob,
And on her whither'd dewlap pour the ale.
The wisest aunt, telling the saddest tale,
Some time for three-foot stool mistaketh me;
Then slip I from her bum, down topples she,
And "tailor" cries, and falls into a cough;
And then the whole quire hold their hips and loff,
And waxen in their mirth, and neeze, and swear
A merry hour was never wasted there.

WILLIAM SHAKESPEARE (1564-1616) from *A Midsummer Night's Dream*

## OBERON

HIS belt was made of Mirtle leaves
Pleyted in small Curious theaves
Besett with Amber Cowslip studdes
And fring'd a bout with daysie budds
In which his Bugle horne was hunge
Made of the Babling Echos tungue
Which sett unto his moone-burnt lippes
Hee windes, and then his fayries skipps.

SIMON STEWARD "Oberon's Apparell: A description of
the King of Fairies Clothes, brought to him on New Yeares Day in
the morning, 1626, by his Queens chambermaids" (1635)

## THE LADY OF THE LAKE

AND there I saw mage Merlin, whose vast wit
And hundred winters are but as the hands
Of loyal vassals toiling for their liege.
And near him stood the Lady of the Lake,
Who knows a subtler magic than his own –
Clothed in white samite, mystic, wonderful.
She gave the King his huge cross-hilted sword,
Whereby to drive the heathen out: a mist
Of incence curled about her, and her face
Wellnigh was hidden in the minster gloom;
But there was heard among the holy hymns
A voice as of the waters, for she dwells
Down in a deep; calm, whatsoever storms
May shake the world, and when the surface rolls,
Hath power to walk the waters like our Lord.

ALFRED, LORD TENNYSON (1809-92) from *Idylls of the King*

# QUEEN MAB

O, then, I see Queen Mab hath been with you.
She is the fairies' midwife; and she comes
In shape no bigger than an agate-stone
On the fore-finger of an alderman,
Drawn with a team of little atomies
Athwart men's noses as they lie asleep.
Her wagon-spokes made of long spinners' legs;
The cover, of the wings of grasshoppers;
The traces, of the smallest spiders' web;
The collars, of the moonshine's watery beams;
Her whip, of cricket's bone; the lash, of film;
Her wagoner, a small grey-coated gnat,
Not half so big as a round little worm
Prick'd from the lazy finger of a maid;
Her chariot is an empty hazel-nut,
Made by the joiner squirrel or old grub,
Time out o' mind the fairies' coachmakers.

WILLIAM SHAKESPEARE (1564-1616) from *Romeo and Juliet*

## TOM THUMBE

Том Thumbe, being thus by miracle begot & borne, in lesse than foure minutes grew to be a little man against which time the Queene of Fayres, his kind Midwife & good Godmother, provided him a very artificiall sute of apparell. First, a Hat made of an oaken leafe, with one feather of a Tittimouse tayle sticking in the same for a plume; his Band and Shirt being both sowed together, was made of a Spiders Cobweb, only for lightnesse and soft wearing for his body: his Cloth for his Doublet and Hose the tenth part of dramme of Thistledowne weaved together: his Stockings the outward Rinde of a greene Apple: his Garters two little hayres pulled from his Mothers eyebrowes.

RICHARD JOHNSON (1573-1659?) from *The History of Tom Thumbe*

# CHAPTER TWO

# Fairy Tricks and Good Turns

*It is not so long ago since country people in much
of the world believed in the existence
of both kindly and mischievous fairies. Brownies
and pixies who came out at night to
help about the house were left thank you gifts by
grateful humans. The goblins and
sprites who led travellers astray and turned the
milk sour, however, were unwanted
visitors kept away by magic charms and
objects, such as a four-leaved clover.*

IF ye will with *Mab* find grace,
Set each Platter in his place:
Rake the Fier up, and get
Water in, ere Sun be set.
Wash your Pailes and clense your Dairies;
Sluts are loathsome to the Fairies:
Sweep your house: Who doth not so,
*Mab* will pinch her by the toe.

ROBERT HERRICK (1591-1674)

from *The Fairies*

*The Nisse of Scandinavia are little people with pointed red caps who are much in evidence around Christmas time. It is believed that they bring the presents under the Christmas tree. In return, children leave a bowl of porridge outside the door for them, and by morning every drop will have gone.*

*The Brownies are the helpful fairies of Scotland
and northern England. Small secretive
people, with brown skin and brown clothes, they
come out at night to do the housework
and make themselves useful about house and farm.*

In the mountains of Switzerland, when
something goes missing it is the Servan who gets
the blame. This little man, no more
than 50 cm high, lives in people's houses and likes
to cause mischief. Not only does he steal,
he also pulls the quilt off the bed while the
occupants are asleep, ties together the
tails of the cows and has even been known to pick
up a horse and put it on the roof.
Leave the Servan a bowl of soup or cream at night,
however, and he will happily sweep the
floor, mind the animals and make sure that the
crops grow large and fine.

I have been smoothing sick folk's pillows, and whispering sweet dreams into their ears; opening cottage casements, to let out the stifling air; coaxing little children away from gutters, and foul pools where fever breeds; turning women from the gin-shop door, and staying men's hands as they were going to strike their wives; doing all I can to help those who will not help themselves; and little enough it is, and weary work for me.

CHARLES KINGSLEY (1819-75) from *The Water Babies*

OBERON:

THROUGH the house give glimmering light,
By the dead and drowsy fire;
Every elf and fairy sprite
Hop as light as bird from brier;
And this ditty, after me,
Sing and dance it trippingly.

TITANIA:

FIRST rehearse your song by rote,
To each word a warbling note;
Hand in hand, with fairy grace,
Will we sing, and bless this place.

WILLIAM SHAKESPEARE (1564-1616)

from *A Midsummer Night's Dream*

# CHAPTER THREE

# Fairy Processions, Feasts and Sports

*Deep in the woods and out on the moors,
fairies like to indulge in their favourite pastimes of
music-making, dancing and hunting.
The more noble among them also hold magnificent
banquets and display their finery in
rides and cavalcades. These activities are a private
pleasure, however, and mortals who
stumble across them by accident often have to
run for their lives.*

Up the airy mountain,
Down the rushy glen
We daren't go a-hunting
For fear of little men;
Wee folk, good folk
Trooping all together;
Green jacket, red cap
And white owl's feather!

Down along the rocky shore
Some make their home
They live on crispy pancakes
Of yellow-tide foam;
Some in the reeds
Of the black mountain-lake
With frogs for their watchdogs,
All night awake.

WILLIAM ALLINGHAM (1824-89) from *The Fairies*

Of which that Britons speken greet honour,
Al was this land fulfild of fayerye,
The elf-queen, with hir joly companye,
Daunced ful ofte in many a grene mede;
This was the old opinion, as I rede.

GEOFFREY CHAUCER (1340?-1400)

"The Wife of Bath's Tale" from *Canterbury Tales*

*Among the Aboriginal Dieri people of
Australia, it was believed that the whirls of dust
which spring up suddenly in the bush were
created by marching armies of fairies whom they
called Kutchi.*

Faery elves,
Whose midnight revels by a forest-side
Or fountain, some belated peasant sees,
Or dreams he sees, while overhead the Moon
Sits arbitress, and nearer to the Earth
Wheels her pale course, they on their mirth
and dance
Intent, with jocund music charm his air.

JOHN MILTON (1608-74) from *Paradise Lost*, Book 1, ll.781-8

*The circles of dark green grass known*
*as fairy rings are said to appear wherever fairies*
*dance. If you run round such a ring nine*
*times on the night of the full moon you may be able*
*to hear them talking and laughing. However,*
*you must remember to run clockwise.*
*Go the other way and the little people will have*
*you in their power.*

THERE was never a merry world since the fairies left off dancing and the Parson left off conjuring.

JOHN SELDEN (1584-1654) from *Table Talk*

ROUND and round the tree of gold,
Round and round dance we.
So doth the great world spin from of old
Summer and winter, and fire and cold,
Song that is sung and tale that is told,
Even as we dance, that fold and unfold
Round the stem of the fairy tree!

ANDREW LANG (1844-1912)

from "The Terrible Head"

# CHAPTER FOUR

# Fairy Homes

As the inhabitants of a kind of
parallel universe, fairies were to be found almost
everywhere, in houses and fields, in the
mountains and the sea, even in the mines from
which men dug out valuable minerals. But
fairyland itself was a magical place, where time
passed at a different pace, and
any mortals who ate food there
became fairies themselves and were
forced to remain for ever.

HERE in cool grot and mossy cell,
We rural fays and fairies dwell;
Though rarely seen by mortal eye,
When pale moon, ascending high,
Darts through yon limes her quivering beams,
We frisk it near these crystal streams.

WILLIAM SHENSTONE (1714-63)

lines inscribed on a tablet in the grounds at the poet's residence

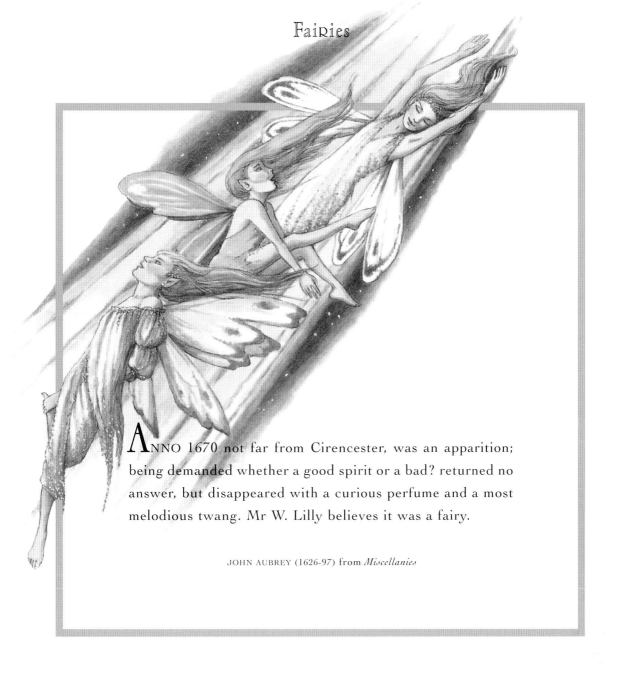

Anno 1670 not far from Cirencester, was an apparition; being demanded whether a good spirit or a bad? returned no answer, but disappeared with a curious perfume and a most melodious twang. Mr W. Lilly believes it was a fairy.

JOHN AUBREY (1626-97) from *Miscellanies*

IN the waning summer light
Which the hearts of mortals love,
'Tis the hour for elfin sprite,
Through the flow'ry mead to rove.

Mortal eyes the spot may scan,
Yet our forms they ne'er descry,
Though so near the haunts of man,
Merrily our trade we ply.

Ever mid the fragrant flowers,
With the songster birds and bees,
Practise we our magic powers
Loving playmates such as these.

EDWARD KNATCHBULL HUGESSEN (1829-93), from *Charlie among the Elves*

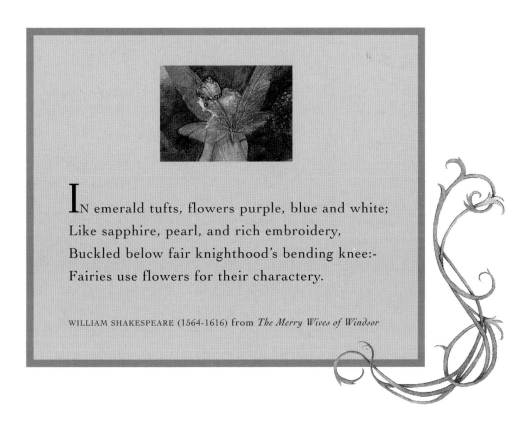

IN emerald tufts, flowers purple, blue and white;
Like sapphire, pearl, and rich embroidery,
Buckled below fair knighthood's bending knee:-
Fairies use flowers for their charactery.

WILLIAM SHAKESPEARE (1564-1616) from *The Merry Wives of Windsor*

’TIS merry, ’tis merry, in Fairy-land
When fairy birds are singing,
When the court doth ride by their monarch's side,
With bit and bridle ringing;

And gaily shines the fairy land
But all is glistening show,
Like the idle gleam that December's beam
Can dart on ice and snow.

SIR WALTER SCOTT (1771-1832) from *The Lady of the Lake*

# CHAPTER FIVE

# Fairy Lovers

*Many tales are told of love and marriage*
*between mortals and fairies and of the wonderfully*
*gifted children they bore. But not all*
*such stories had happy endings. Wherever they*
*chose to live, in fairyland or on earth, one*
*of the two lovers would often pine for the home they*
*had abandoned and eventually*
*return there alone, leaving husbands*
*and wives to mourn for ever.*

HITHER come hither and see;
And the rainbow hangs on the poising wave,
And sweet is the colour of cove and cave,
And sweet shall your welcome be:
O hither, come hither, and be our lords
For merry brides are we:
We will kiss sweet kisses, and speak sweet words:
O listen, listen, your eyes shall glisten
With pleasure and love and jubilee.

ALFRED, LORD TENNYSON (1809-92)

"The Sea Fairies"

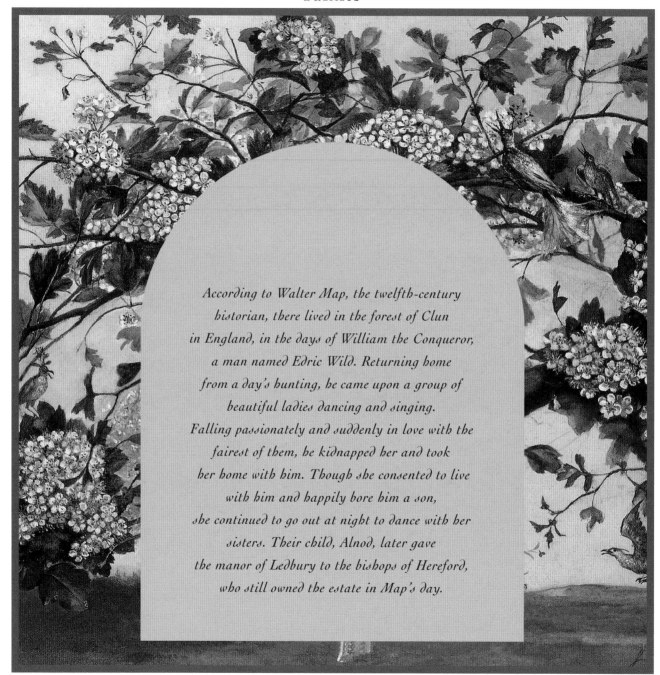

According to Walter Map, the twelfth-century
historian, there lived in the forest of Clun
in England, in the days of William the Conqueror,
a man named Edric Wild. Returning home
from a day's hunting, he came upon a group of
beautiful ladies dancing and singing.
Falling passionately and suddenly in love with the
fairest of them, he kidnapped her and took
her home with him. Though she consented to live
with him and happily bore him a son,
she continued to go out at night to dance with her
sisters. Their child, Alnod, later gave
the manor of Ledbury to the bishops of Hereford,
who still owned the estate in Map's day.

MOST goodly glee and lovely blandishment
She made to me, and bad me love her deare,
For dearly sure her love was to me bent,
As, when just time expired, should appear.
But, whether dreams delude or true it were,
Was never heart so ravish'd with delight,
No living man like words did ever hear,
As she to me delivered all that night;
And at her parting said, she Queen of Faeries hight.

EDMUND SPENSER (1552?-1599) from *The Faerie Queene*

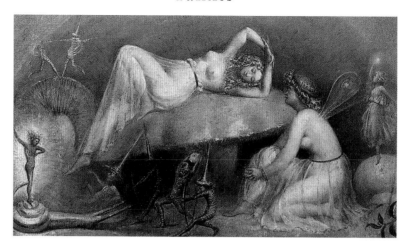

Melusine, the best known of French fairies,
was condemned to become a serpent every Saturday.
The Count of Lusignan fell in love with
her, but she would only agree to marry him on
condition that he never visited her on a Saturday.
Eventually, full of jealousy and suspicion,
the Count broke his promise and Melusine was
compelled to leave him and to wander the
world as a ghost. The cry she gave when she saw
her husband on that fateful day gave rise
to the French phrase, un cri de Melusine; a shriek
of despair. Even after the castle of the
Lusignan family became the property of the French
king, she continued to appear, both in
human and in snake form, until the building was
destroyed in the sixteenth century.

# Fairies

King Orfeo was the best harper in the world. He ruled the
kingdom of Tracyens and was happily married to the beautiful Queen
Meroudys. One May Day while Meroudys was sleeping
under an apple tree the king of the fairies spirited her away. Orfeo was like a
man distracted, and when no trace of Meroudys could be found
he called his nobles together and appointed his steward regent. Barefoot and
in rags he went out into the wilderness with only his harp.
For ten years he lived in the wilderness taming the beasts with his beautiful
music and searching for his queen.

One day he heard the sound of horns and a troop of fairy knights
rode past him; among them he saw Meroudys. Orfeo followed, running as fast
as their horses could gallop, through a cleft in the rock and
into a fairy country with a shining palace. Claiming a minstrel's right of
entry Orfeo was admitted into the fairy king's presence
and given permission to play. From every room in the palace the fairies
poured in to listen and at the end of the music when the king
promised him any boon he asked, Orfeo asked for the lady asleep under the
apple tree. "That would be a foul coupling", said the fairy king,
"she so fair and gentle and you so rough and ragged". "Yet it would be a
fouler thing", said Orfeo, "for a great king to break his promise made
before all his knights." "You are a brave man," said the king. "Take her with
you." So the two returned joyfully to their home where the steward
had ruled loyally and well. They were welcomed back with true joy and lived
out their lives in great happiness.

TRUE Thomas lay on Huntlie bank;
A marvel he did see;
For there he saw a lady bright,
Come riding down by the Eildon tree.

Her skirt was of the grass-green silk,
Her mantle of the velvet fine;
On every lock of her horse's mane,
Hung fifty bells and nine.

True Thomas he pulled off his cap,
And bowed low down on his knee;
"All hail, thou mighty Queen of Heaven!
For thy peer on earth never could be."

"O no, O no, Thomas," she said.
"That name does not belong to me;
I'm but the Queen of fair Elfland,
That hither am come to visit thee.

"Harp and carp, Thomas," she said,
"Harp and carp along with me;
And if ye dare to kiss my lips,
Sure of your body I will be!"

"Betide me weal, betide me woe,
That weird shall never daunten me!"
Then he has kissed her on the lips,
All underneath the Eildon tree.

ANONYMOUS BALLAD, possibly sixteenth century

# Fairies

# ACKNOWLEDGEMENTS

The following pictures are reproduced with kind permission of the Bridgeman Art Library, London:

p2: *The Marriage of Oberon and Titania* by John Anster Fitzgerald, private collection. p3 & 24: *The elf attendant on Bottom*, illustration to "A Midsummer Night's Dream", by Arthur Rackham, private collection. p5 & 27: *Little Girl with Fairies* by Beatrice Goldsmith, Chris Beetles Ltd, London. p6 (detail): *A Fairy Song* from "A Midsummer Night's Dream", by Arthur Rackham, Spencer Collection, New York Public Library. p7: *Twilight Dreams* by Arthur Rackham, University of Liverpool Art Gallery & Collections. p8: *The Fairy Queen* by Richard Painton, Fine-Lines (Fine Art), Warwickshire. p10: *"The Fairy's Tightrope"* from Peter Pan in Kensington Gardens by JM Barrie by Arthur Rackham, private collection. p13: *Faun and the Fairies* by Daniel Maclise, private collection. p14: *The Lamentation of King Arthur* by William Bell Scott, Whitford & Hughes, London. p15: *The Taking of Excalibur* by John McKirdy Duncan, City of Edinburgh Museums and Art Galleries. p17: *Queen Mab*, 1860 by George Cruikshank, Forbes Magazine Collection, London. p20: *Puck* by Sir Joshua Reynolds, private collection. p21: *The Enchanted Forest*, 1886 by Sir John Gilbert, Guildhall Art Gallery, Corporation of London. p22/3: *Triumphal March of the Elf King* by Richard Doyle, British Library, London. p26: *Tommelise very desolate on the water lily leaf in "Thumbkinetta"* from Hans Christian Andersen's Fairy Tales, 1872 by Eleanor Vere Boyle, Victoria and Albert Museum, London. p28: *"She found herself face to face with a stately and beautiful lady"* from "Beauty and the Beast" by Edmund Dulac, Victoria and Albert Museum, London. p29: *Spellbound* by Frederick George Cotman, Christopher Wood Gallery, London. p30 & 33 (details): *Cock Robin defending his Nest* by John Anster Fitzgerald, private collection. p31: *The Quarrel of Oberon and Titania*, 1849 by Sir Joseph Noel Paton, National Gallery of Scotland, Edinburgh. p38: *Fairy Dance*, 1882 by William Holmes Sullivan, private collection. p39: *Watching the Fairies*, 1925 by Beatrice Goldsmith, Chris Beetles Ltd, London.

p41: *Come, now a Roundel* by Arthur Rackham, Chris Beetles Ltd, London. p42 & 47 (details): *Fairies in a Nest* by John Anster Fitzgerald, The Maas Gallery, London. p43: *Nocturnal Spires* by Edmund Dulac, Victoria and Albert Museum, London. p48: *Fairy and sprites in the undergrowth* by Georges Picard, private collection. p52/3: *Come unto these yellow sands*, 1842 by Richard Dadd, private collection. p54: *Ariel* by John Anster Fitzgerald, Walker Art Gallery, Liverpool. p55: *Titania* by John Simmons, City of Bristol Museum and Art Gallery. p56/7: *There Sleeps Titania* by John Simmons, private collection. p58: *Fairy resting on a Mushroom* by Thomas Heatherley, private collection. p58: *The Fairy Wood* by Henry Maynell Rheam, Roy Miles Gallery, 29 Bruton Street, London W1.

The Visual Arts Library, London:

p32: *Vernon: The Fairy Haunt*, private collection. p46: (arch) *Danby*, Fairies, Leicester Galleries, London. p50: *Emslie*, Shakespeare ou le bacon, Leicester Galleries, London. p59: *Barker*, The Spirit of the Sun, private collection. p62: *Fuseli, La Reine des Fees apparait au Prince Arthur*, Goethe Museum, Frankfurt).

Fine Art Photographs:

Front jacket: *Midsummer Eve* by Edward Robert Hughes, RWS. Back jacket: *The Lily Fairy* by Luis Ricardo Falero. Half title & p49: *Spirit of the Night* by Grimshaw. p8/9: *Titania* by Michael. p19: *Titania and the Indian Boy* by Paton. p25: *The Time I've Lost in Wooing* by Maclise. p34: *A Glimpse of the Fairies* by Lear. p46 (top): *A Midsummer Night's Dream* by Paton. p46: (bottom) *Titania Asleep – Midsummer Night's Dream* by Naish. p51: *Hermia and Lysander* (from Shakespear's "Midsummer Night's Dream") by Simmons. p63: *Thomas the Rhymer and the Queen of the Faerie* by Paton.

The Arthur Rackham pictures are reproduced with the Kind Permission of His Family